HeartSongs

Written and Illustrated by Matthew Joseph Thaddeus Stepanek
"Mattie"

VSP Books

HYPERION

New York

ISBN: 0-7868-8809-1

Hyperion books are available for special promotions and premiums.
For details contact Hyperion Special Markets, 77 West 66th Street,
11th floor, New York, New York, 10023, or call 212-456-0100.

FIRST EDITION

10 9 8 7 6 5 4 3 2 1

CONTENTS

Dedication

This book is dedicated to those who believe in celebrating the gifts of life every day, especially my mom, all of my kin, and the entire staff of the Pediatric Intensive Care Unit at Children's National Medical Center. Always remember to play after every storm!

Stevie

Jamie

Mattie

Katie

Senses 5

Making Real Sense of the Senses

Our eyes are for looking at things,
But they are also for crying
When we are very happy or very sad.
Our ears are for listening,
But so are our hearts.
Our noses are for smelling food,
But also the wind and the grass and
If we try very hard, butterflies.
Our hands are for feeling,
But also for hugging and touching so gently.
Our mouths and tongues are for tasting,
But also for saying words, like
"I love you," and
"Thank you, God, for all of these things."

The Gift of Color

Thank You
For all the colors of the rainbow.
Thank You
For sharing these colors
With all of the fish
And all of the birds
And all of the flowers
That You have given us.
And thank You
For the colors of the
Heaven-in-the-earth
And of the
Heaven-in-the-sky,
And for sharing these colors
In the people of the world.
You give us color
As a gift, God,
And I thank You
For all of these
Beautiful colors and
Beautiful things and
Beautiful people.
What special gifts
You have given to us!

The Smell of a Noise

Shhhh...
I smell something.
It smells like a noise.
Like a turtle noise.
Yes, that's what it is.
It is a turtle noise,
And it is wonderful,
Because turtles
Live inside of seashells.
Would you like to
Live in a seashell?
It would smell like
A turtle noise,
But I think
It would be wonderful!

Angel-Wings

This morning,
I smelled something very good.
Perhaps,
It was a rainbow.
Or maybe,
It was a dinosaur smile.
Or even,
A seashell.
I am not sure
What I smelled.
And I am not sure
What rainbows
Or dinosaur smiles
Or seashells
Smell like.
But I'm sure they smell wonderful.
Wonderful and special
Like the smell of
Angel-Wings.
But also,
I'm sure they smell
A little sad,
Because we can't really smell
A rainbow,
Or a dinosaur smile,
Or a seashell,
Or especially,
We can't really smell
The wonderful smell
Of Angel-Wings.

Very Special Candy

One day,
I will make a bag of
Very Special Candy.
The candy will come in
All different colors,
Colors like you see in
Good Ordinary Candy.
But...
The flavors will be
So different and
So special and
So wonderful.
There will be little
Blue candies
That taste like sky.
And the little
Green and brown candies
Will taste like grass and trees.
The orange ones
Will taste like butterfly,
The yellow ones
Like flowers and sunshine,
And the white ones
Like clouds in Heaven.
And then,
I will make a very, very
Special piece of candy,
That is all different colors
And that glows like a halo.
And that will be the one
That tastes like
Rainbow and Angels.

When My Feet Itch

When my feet itch,
Maybe I'll think about
Riding on a dinosaur
With my mom —
And then,
I won't remember that my feet itch.
When my feet itch,
Maybe I'll think about
Spending the night at the
North Pole with Santa Claus —
And then,
It will be too cold for my feet to itch.
When my feet itch,
Maybe I'll think about
Playing with Nick and Ben
Because they're some of the
Best friends a kid could ever have —
And then,
I won't care if my feet itch or not.
Or maybe, when my feet itch,
I'll think about Angels —
Because they don't make
You itch when you touch them.

Seasons 12

Leaf for a Day

Today,
I think I will be a tree.
Or perhaps,
A leaf on a branch on the tree.
I will feel
The gentle breeze,
And then I will
`Plip' off of my branch and my tree
And float in the wind.
I will go
Back and forth in the breeze
All the way down to the ground.
And after I rest
And say `hello'
To the grass and dirt and bugs,
I will call to the wind,
`Come and take me
To visit my other leaf-friends
On all of the other trees, please.'
And the gentle breeze
Will come
And pick me up
So that I can jump and dance
With all of the other
Tree-stars and tree-flowers
That God gave the world.
What a special idea
To be, today.

On the Mountain of Tree-Stars

Summer is almost over.
Soon, it will be September,
And then, it will be fall.
And when it is fall,
We can play with all
The tree-stars that fall
To us from up high.
And when the tree-stars fall
From the sky,
We can build a leaf-mountain.
First, when all
The leaves fall
From the sky,
We put them all
Together into a mountain-pile
Way up high.
Then, we get a string and tie
Them all
Together so that when
The wind blows they won't fly
Away from the mountain-pile.
And last, we climb
Up the leaf-mountain,
And we stand up so high
Next to the sky,
And then —- sliiiiiiide —-
We slide
Aaaaaaaaalll
The way to the bottom of the mountain-leaf pile.
So when the fall
Comes it will get chilly,
And things will start to fall
Like the season.
But they don't fall
With a boom!
Only they fall
Like a floating leaf, or
Like a little boy on
The Mountain of Tree-Stars.

Winter Luck

Snowflakes...
They come down so slow,
And sometimes so fast,
Looking like pretty stars
Falling down, down, down
To the ground.
Little stars with little holes,
Bigger stars with bigger holes,
They are all cuddly snowflake stars.
Snowflakes of the tiny snows,
Snowstars of the bigger snows,
I will catch you on my hand
Or on my tongue
And make a wish...
I will make a wish on
My falling snowstar,
And then have good luck
All day, all night, all Ever.

Important Things

When I grow up,
I think maybe
I will be a snowman,
Because when it
Snows outside,
I'll already be cold
And like it.
And children will
Play with me,
And laugh
And sing
And dance
All around me.
And those are important
Things to have happen
When you grow up.

16

Indian Winter

Hey!
It's cold out here today!
This is May,
And it's supposed to be
Spring
Turning into
Summer,
So I can have my birthday.
But I need my jacket,
And my hat.
Oh, bother!
I wonder —-
Who played with the seasons
Last night
While we were all sleeping?

The Eye of the Beholder

Dandelions are NOT weeds!
See?
They have beautiful
Yellow flowers on them.
They have lovely
Green stems.
Mommy puts them
In a jar of water
In the kitchen —-
They are flowers!
See?
They are round.
They are round and yellow.
Oh, mommy,
Please tell him
He's making a big mistake!
Poor little dandelions...
He's pulling them all up
And calling them "weeds."
Oh, this is
So horrible, so sad!
What would God say if
He saw you sending all of these
Poor, little, round, yellow
Dandelion-flowers
Back to the Lord?

Summer 'Rememberies'

After everyone has
A smoky cookout at Chip's house,
And the grown-ups make
Music on their guitars for singing and dancing,
And the children take
Off their shoes and run
Around the backyard catching
Lightning bugs in the dark —-
Then, it is a very good time to be
Happy.
And that `then' is
A very good time and
A very good feeling to remember
Ever-after.

Celebrations 20

The Importance of Windows

Windows are very good things to have.
They let you look out,
And see all the different things.
And they let you look in,
To see all the other different things.
And do you know what is the most
Special window of all?
The window in your heart,
That's between the Heaven-in-the-earth,
And the Heaven-in-the-sky.

Circle of Happiness

I am a little kid
For you to love.
I am a little kid
For you to hug and kiss.
I am a little kid
For you to say,
"You are so special,
Yes you are" to.
I am a little kid
For all of those things
And more.
And when you
Feel and say and do
All of those things,
I will be a little kid
Who will love you.
I will be a little kid
Who will hug and kiss you.
I will be a little kid
Who will say to you,
"You are so special, too,
Yes you are."
I will be a little kid
Who will do all of those things
And more.
And that is what
Happiness
Is all about.

On Being Thankful

Dear God,
I was going to thank You tonight
For a beautiful sunrise,
That was pink behind the fog down the hill,
And for a wonderful rainbow,
That I ran under pointing to
All my favorite colors,
And for such a great sunset,
That sparkled orange across the water.
I was going to thank You tonight
For all of these special gifts,
Except that none of them happened.
But do You know what?
I still love You, God,
And I have lots of other things
That I can thank You for tonight,
Even if you didn't give those
Very special gifts to me today.
It's okay, God,
Because I'll look for them all again,
When my tomorrow comes.
Amen.

Pinch of Peace

Dear God,
Tonight my prayers are for the world.
We have to stop this fighting.
We have to stop the wars.
People need to lay down their weapons,
And find peace in their hearts.
People need to stop arguing and hating.
People need to notice the good things.
People need to remember You, God.
Maybe You could come and
Shoot a little bow-and-arrow pinch
Into all the angry peoples' hearts, God.
Then they would feel You again.
And then they would realize what
They are doing and how horrible the
Killing and hating and fighting is,
And they might even begin to pray.
Then, they could reach in, and
Pull the little bow-and-arrow pinch
Out of their hearts and feel good
And be loving and living people again.
And then,
The world would be at peace, and
The children would be safe, and
The people would be happy, and
We could all say "thank You" together.
Amen.

Heartsong

I have a song, deep in my heart,
And only I can hear it.
If I close my eyes and sit very still
It is so easy to listen to my song.
When my eyes are open and
I am so busy and moving and busy,
If I take time and listen very hard,
I can still hear my Heartsong.
It makes me feel happy.
Happier than ever.
Happier than everywhere
And everything and everyone
In the whole wide world.
Happy like thinking about
Going to Heaven when I die.
My Heartsong sounds like this —-
    I love you! I love you!
    How happy you can be!
    How happy you can make
    This whole world be!
And sometimes it's other
Tunes and words, too,
But it always sings the
Same special feeling to me.
It makes me think of
Jamie, and Katie and Stevie,
And other wonderful things.
This is *my* special song.
But do you know what?
All people have a special song
Inside their hearts!
Everyone in the whole wide world
Has a special Heartsong.
If you believe in magical, musical hearts,
And if you believe you *can* be happy,
Then you, too, will hear *your* song.

The Daily Gift

You know what?
Tomorrow is a new day.
And today is a new day.
Actually,
Every day is a new day.
Thank You, God,
For all of these
Special and new days.

About the Author

I am Mattie J.T. Stepanek.
My body has light skin,
Red blood, blue eyes, and blond hair.
Since I have mitochondrial myopathy,
I even have a trach, a ventilator, and oxygen.
Very poetic, I am, and very smart, too.
I am always brainstorming ideas and stories.
I am a survivor, but some day, I will see
My two brothers and one sister in Heaven.
When I grow up, I plan to become
A daddy, a writer, a public speaker,
And most of all, a peacemaker.
Whoever I am, and whatever happens,
I will always love my body and mind,
Even if it has different abilities
Than other peoples' bodies and minds.
I will always be happy, because
I will always be me.

Eleven-year-old Matthew Joseph Thaddeus Stepanek, best known as "Mattie," has been writing poetry and short stories since age three. Mattie's poems have been published in a variety of mediums and he has been an invited speaker for several seminars, conferences and television shows. In 1999, he was awarded the Melinda Lawrence International Book Award for inspirational written works by the Children's Hospice International. He has appeared on *Oprah*, *The Today Show*, *Good Morning America* and many other programs. In addition to writing, Mattie enjoys reading, collecting rocks and shells, and playing with Legos. He has earned a black belt in martial arts, and in 2001, Mattie served as the Maryland State Goodwill Ambassador for the Muscular Dystrophy Association. In 2002, he will serve as both the National Ambassador and the State Ambassador for the MDA. He lives with his mother, Jeni, in Upper Marlboro, MD, where he is home-schooled.

© Jim Hawkins

The publishers wish to acknowledge the assis-
tance and support of the following people in the pro-
duction of this book: Martha Shaw Whitley, our amaz-
ing sister, for organizing and coordinating the people
and events which allow Mattie's book to be shared far
and wide; Marissa L. Garis, public relations and market-
ing specialist at Children's National Medical Center for
introducing us to Mattie and his mom, Jeni, and giving
us the opportunity to publish Mattie's poems; Catherine
Morrison, our production director, who tries to keep us
all organized; and Jeni Stepanek, Mattie's mom, whose
hidden talents as an editor are greatly appreciated.

Peter and Cheryl Barnes
VSP Books
Alexandria, Virginia
June 2001